Where Do We Go from Here?

Poetry and artwork
by
Maria Alexandria Boyd Paddock

EARTHWild

EarthWild Publishing
1999

This book was typeset in Times New Roman, 14 pt. italic.
Printed on recycled paper.

Paddock, Maria Alexandria, 1967 -
Where do we go from here?
First edition.

ISBN 0-9672023-0-2
1. poetry. I. Paddock, Maria. II. Title.

Illustrations, photographs, and
book design by Maria A. Paddock

EarthWILD Publishing
7116 Stinson Ave. #A208
Gig Harbor, WA. 98335
To order: (253) 853-6144

printed by:
Valley Press
Puyallup, WA.
(800) 926-4685

This book is dedicated to my mother, Donna Boyd, and to my husband, Rod Paddock, because they have inspired me, loved me, and supported me, and because they are my best friends.

Contents

Summer

Redwinged blackbird's call
scrapes musically against
quiet cattail pond.

Friends Remembering

Time was when we were children,
wondering of things unknown,
where knowledge had not yet been sown.

We were friends forever,
playing together...
Remember?

Our own little world was spinning -
so long we could not remember a beginning.
We were always together...

Wherever you went, I went.
Wherever I went, you would follow.
Everything we saw and did was together.

We were friends forever,
loving together...
Remember?

From a Seat on the Bed

Isolation.
The cat
and a crow.
The fan
catches dust.
Outside
it's been raining,
and the carpet
is crooked.
And my tennis shoes
are waiting
for something.

A stack of books
on the floor
and a bag
of blue yarn.
Animals sleeping
in the dark,
warm like the laundry
heaped in a pile.
And one tennis shoe
steps on the other,
bashfully wanting to play.

Animal Choices

Why does a fish
swim where it does?
How does a bee
choose where to buzz?
Currents, gradients,
a search for what's new?
Or a simple desire
to take in the view?

Favorite Times

It's the quiet times I like the best,
the chatting times,
the friendly times,
when inside feelings can come out.
That time when people can come close
and share themselves.
My favorite time is when
you find out that someone
is your brother,
but God just forgot
to give you the same parents.

Shared Sky

Our worlds are not as separate as we might think.
What we do here affects all other lives on this planet.
Shared sky.
Shared planet.
We are all in this together.

Morning

Up at 7:30 a.m.
The house is filled with grey
in the early morning light.
The dog is pacing, restless,
but otherwise, all is still.
The house is quiet, empty,
and the only sign I find
that my husband was still here
less than a moment ago
is the hot water waiting
to flow immediately
from the blue bathroom faucet
as I start to wash my face.

Skipping Stones

I went to the beach today with my grandfather.
He's been dead for almost 20 years,
but he was with me today.
I feel him standing close to me,
smiling,
and I hope he's really here
and not just in my mind.
Of course, he's in my heart.
He's always in my heart.

We walked along the sloping shore,
watching pebbles approach our feet.
I don't know that my grandfather and I
ever skipped stones together,
but we did today.
I found flat, dark, round stones -
the flat ones are always dark here -
turned my left side to the water
and sent the stones skittering across its surface.
Grandfather's hand was my hand,
the twist of his side in the twist of mine -
but he was also just behind me -
watching and smiling,
and laughing at my joy
from quick leaping stones.

How wet does a skipping stone get
before it hops its last hop?
Before it begins its run (or plunge),
it might be dry or wet.
It is momentarily warmed
by the hand that launches it.
Then, I think, with each skip,
it cools just a little
and accustoms itself to the water -
just as you and I get into the pool
one inch at a time.
Those rocks that don't skip
would just dive right in,
if they were people.
Therefore, round rocks seem less thoughtful,
more deliberative.
I like the slow smoothness
of the flat rock in my hand.

And if you took all the sun-warmed,
then hand-warmed, flat, black rocks off the
beach
and skipped them towards Neptune,
so they went all at once,
would their warmth kiss the surface
and warm the ocean's cool toes?

These are the things I'd ask of my grandfather -
light-hearted and whimsy -

basked in laughter and sunshine.
But his presence is like sunlight -
glowing but silent,
and so close yet just out of reach.
If you stand quiet and still,
you can feel the sun wrap around you,
but turn to embrace the light,
and your arms pass right through.

I wish he were here -
with his hugs and his voice -
so I could tell him how much
I enjoyed this day with him.
So we could chat
about stones meeting water.
But even the best skipping stone
can only travel so far.
Eventually, it will take its last skip
and sink below the surface,
beyond our reach,
and all that will be left,
as I stand on the shore,
is a sun-sparkled memory
and a lingering warmth in my heart.

Life

The wind in the trees
whispers softly in my heart
songs of colored leaves.

Seven Trees

Seven leaves
in each of seven trees
are turning golden.

Twenty leaves
in twenty trees
have reddened.

A hundred leaves
in as many trees
are turning.

Maple leaves
in maple trees
are falling.

Forest trees
losing leaves
in autumn.

Confusion

Confusion
is opposites presented together.

Happiness
is no longer being opposites.

Forgotten

An apple tossed into an empty lot,
A car sitting in a field to rust,
A dying rose garden going to seed,
An old woman sitting in a crumbling hut,
Living a lonely life and dying -
ignored.

Homeless

I'm a homeless person.
You gave me a wastebasket today.
When you look at me
do you see waste to be thrown away?

My jacket has holes.
My blanket is holes.
My shoes are so holey
they have attained nirvana
and ceased to exist.
Drink keeps me warm
where my blanket does not
and puts holes in my life.

I can't decide if it's better
to live in the holes,
which are blank,
or to live in the pieces
around them.
Which part should I throw away
in the wastebasket?

What's New

The news report at eleven on Channel 5:
"Your local news is next
on this day, Sunday, November 5, 1995."
But it could be any channel on any day
as they bring you an hour
filled with death and violence -
and a smattering of the good and the weird,
if time allows.

Today's top story -
Hundreds gather to mourn the passing of
Yitzhak Rabin
and to pay respect to the slain Israeli leader
whose name stood for peace.
He was a vigilant warrior turned peacemaker,
killed by one who sought
to derail the peace process.
Tears and anger
as solidarity tries to stand against division.

Also in the news -
A convicted child molester is caught
after three years on the run,
named and pictured - on your TV.
In Seattle, a woman and child
dead in their home
with no sign of a struggle.
And elsewhere, an apartment complex burned.

As for the good and the weird -
A 10-year-old birthday girl
decides to give rather than receive.
All birthday guests
are asked to bring food for the homeless.
Stray hairs found in the Northwest mountains,
suspected to have come from Bigfoot,
will undergo DNA analysis -
the first such test in the Bigfoot mystery.

Meanwhile -
The White Salmon River
has become a junkyard
after years of abuse.
The streambed, littered with garbage,
everything from mattresses to cars,
is to be cleaned up by locals
enlisting a helicopter to remove tons of waste
degrading the river.

And in California -
A San Francisco landmark, St. Paul's,
burns to the ground.
More than 150 firefighters fought the blaze
which came off the steeple
and blew out the front doors.
The church, more than 100 years old,
withstood the 1906 earthquake,
but was totally destroyed by this fire.

And in foreign news -
The Philippines is cleaning up
after Typhoon Angela,
their worst storm in 15 years.
More than 500 dead, 280 missing,
and hundreds of thousands made homeless.
Rescue efforts proceed
but are hindered by loss of power
in more than a third of the country.

Other than sports, weather, a few more deaths,
that's today's news.
Except for a change in names and numbers,
it could have been yesterday's news,
or tomorrow's.
And although the loss of Yitzhak Rabin
is more than an everyday occurrence,
the death counts and violence
have become mundane -
typical everyday fare in the news.

"Thank you for watching tonight's broadcast,"
says the anchor,
"We'll see you tomorrow at seven."
The newscasters smile and laugh,
secure in their never-ending job
of reporting tragedies.
They seem unmoved by daily disasters.
But how can we live in a world like this?

Mountains

The mountain remains,
but changes slowly.
People quickly change
and don't remain.

If people were stationary
and mountains wavered,
people would be less interesting,
and mountains less beautiful.

Slipping

Inspiration drips, slips
from my mind.
Or is it Insanity?
Is there a difference?
Or does one beget the other...
I am losing my mind
as it falls on the page
in pieces
that you think are words.
It slips from my head,
flows through my fingers,
becomes one with the pen,
for a moment.
It seeps through the ink
as I lose my mind
to the page.

the Memory of

Remember Us

I visited a graveyard yesterday.
My husband prefers to call them cemeteries,
but I think it's okay to say graveyard
when the stones are all crooked
and leaning against each other from age.
We all need support when we're old
and mind less what people call us.

I walked among grey shale
marking rows six feet apart,
carved with wings, chalices, and skulls
and dates two hundred years past.
The graves of young and old
brought together by death -
some near others for the first time -
some next to kin and beloved.

With no room to walk between,
I gingerly stepped on the graves
but felt allowed to do so
as the ghosts of the past
welcomed my visit, my attention,
pleased to have someone take notice,
to read names long unspoken
by the dusty lips of their friends,
to reassure them that they had lived
and would not be forgotten.

Winter

Electricity
warms my toes curled within
an old blue blanket.

Dragon Cat

A black form hunches by the hearth;
a tail lazily twitches to and fro.
A stretch, a yawn... the form rolls over.

Glowing eyes - like yellow flames;
they glance about the hearth
and settle on an unsuspecting mouse.
Muscles flex, jaws open wide and yawn again.
A crouching figure preparing for a spring
while luminescent eyes dart back and forth.
But no - the muscles relax.

The Dragon Cat waits once more
while his eyes note the leaping flames of fire
and the mouse tracks across the floor.

Refuge

I'm falling skywards,
into blue,
in the open space of freedom,
and reveling in the sunlit snow
that sparkles at my feet.

Above, and beckoning,
the jagged bear teeth of the Rockies
snag imagination wisps
as the crisp forever sky
of a sunny winter day
takes my breath away.
There is power here -
asleep in caves
and waiting on the wind.
And life thrives -
even in the coldest glacier,
where the iceworms dream.
The peaks are feared by some
as the place where spirits dwell,
but I recognize these mountains
as a refuge for our soul,
a home,
where, when we leave our cities,
we can come to find ourselves.
On this mountain made of rock
(and not by human hands)
graced by snowfalls
of one unique flake at a time,
we can follow pine blessed winds
and fleeting wild tracks
to a humbling, awesome place
where the mountains take us skyward
and we can still be free.

Anger

It's a round mass of branches,
A prickly, scraggly ball,
Staunch and unyielding.
The warmth is gone,
The color faded,
With little left but sharp points.

It could be a wintry tree
When the leaves have flown,
The moss has frozen,
And the birds have moved away.
In a way, it's like that,
For it's lonely, too.

But the tree has life inside.
It will blossom again,
Bringing warmth, color,
And softness to its world.

So how can we make anger
More like the tree?

Payment

You came to our village
in your noisy green jeeps,
and you offered us aid
while you bombed our country.

We had rice to eat
and schools for our children,
but you rationed our rice
and you re-roofed our schools.

Your help was insistent
but did not match our needs;
you brought bombs to our land
and VC to our homes.

A small, dusty village,
of peasants and children,
doesn't need shiny new roofs
to attract VC rage.

We tried to say no
and that we cannot pay
"No need, this aid is free
and won't cost you a thing."

No, please, we don't want this.
We are poor but alive.
What we have is enough
so please leave us alone.

"We must help, we will help;
a new roof, it is done.
Your life is now better -
no payment required."

We will pay, be assured.
There is always a cost,
only now it is paid
with our homes and our lives.

We said we could not pay,
but we have and we will.
When they see what we've got,
the VC will come visit.

They'll exact a high price
for the pride that we've shown,
and place rage, hate, and fear
in the eyes of our young.

Then you, who came bringing aid,
will next bring us napalm
as you bomb the VC
to "clean out" our town.

"We're killing the enemy,"
you say as bombs drop,
and "We're just helping you,"
as our grandmothers wail.

Our homes are afire;
the new roof is ablaze;
people lie in pieces
in our once quiet streets.

We've lost all that we had,
except pain and grief.
We have made our payment
with families and children.

* *I respect and honor the sorrows and sacrifices of our soldiers in the Vietnam War. My lament is for the often misguided, though well-intentioned, policies of foreign aid and for the terrible ravages of war inflicted upon innocent victims.*

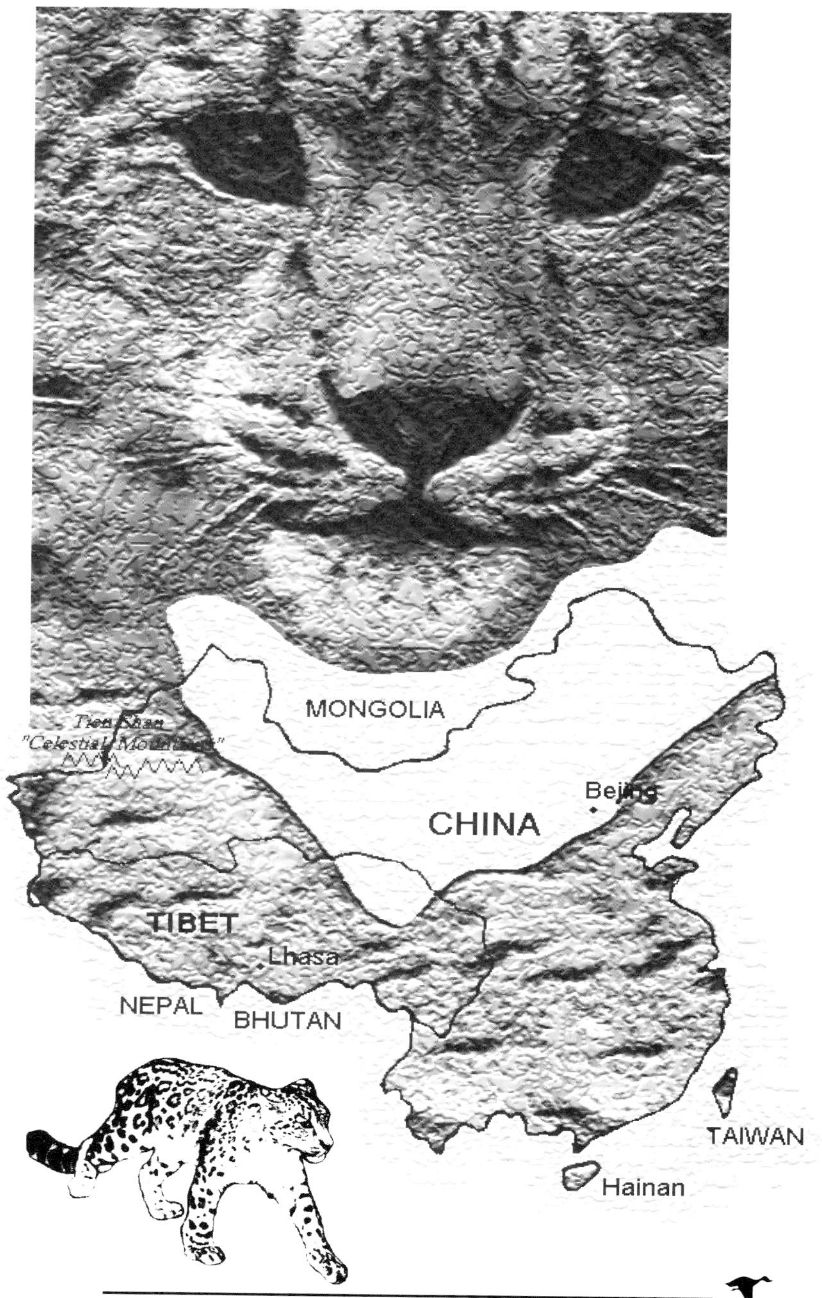

Tien Shan
MONGOLIA
Beijing
CHINA
TIBET
Lhasa
NEPAL
BHUTAN
TAIWAN
Hainan

Tien Shan

Fur
claws
on padded
paws
hold high
a shale-colored
tail
with black rings -
the leopard springs.

In
Asia's old
mountains
cold,
there lives
the rare
endangered pair

of the last
snow leopards
left.

Dark Days

These dark days
of winter
are brightened
only by the reflection
of snow drifts
which
darken your mind
and your heart
as they claim
your trees,
your livestock,
and the roof
over your head,
leaving you
cold and wasted
inside
and waiting
for your soul
to thaw.

The Green and the Black

Two men
grown together
and linked from birth
set out upon a quest.
One tall and thoughtful
who favored green,
his hair tousled by the wind
and feet connected to the earth.
The other strong and bold
in heavy reds and black,
unmoved by elements
he thought he could control.
They journeyed a great distance
to the farthest mountain peak -
a place where men
were said to find great power.
After many hard days travel
they reached the very top.
The man in green
stood quietly
and savored their success
at seeing the world laid out below.
The darker one in black
leapt to the highest rock
and howled in conquering triumph
at owning all within his sight.

The wind whipped by his face
and touched not a single hair
as he smiled to himself
and wondered
"What if I <u>alone</u> were here?"

The mountains' echo ran its course
and his howl reached up behind him -
startled, wheeling toward his friend,
he found just empty space.
Selfish power asked in fear
"What if that happened to me?"
and the wind raced unhindered
across the barren peak.

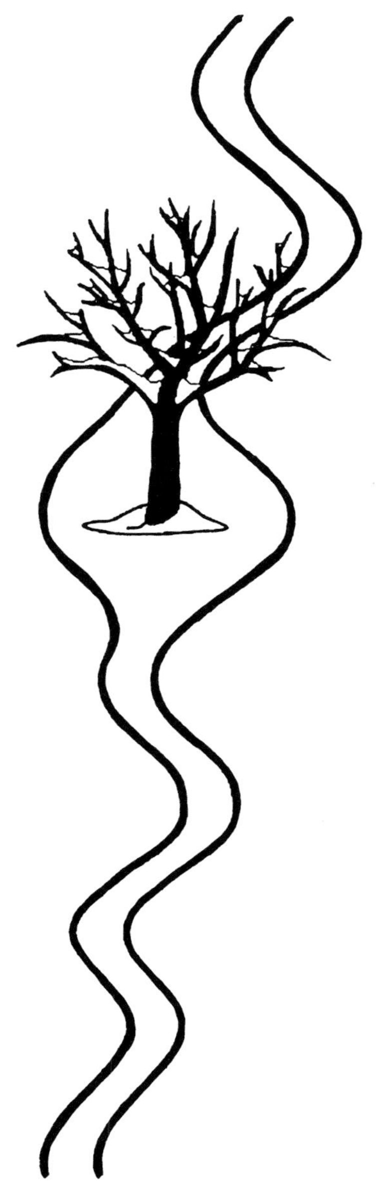

The Trail

She leaves a track
as she makes her way
down the clean, white surface
beneath her trail.

The lines flow smoothly
until she hits a bump.
A jolt, a sudden stop
to ponder.

She eases back gently
as she finds her path
and resumes the rhythm
of writing poetry.

Wild Horses

Forty-seven horses
Are waiting at the gate,
Champing, pawing, snorting,
Impatiently they wait.

The gate falls before
The ponies' wild state,
As I reflect upon my life
And see that it's too late.

Seeking my meaning -
Is it free-will or my fate -
Striving, hoping, reaching,
For something to create.

The effort to live
What life put on my plate,
Birthing, living, dying,
And learning to relate.

I found songs to sing
And thoughts to illustrate
On peace for man and beast
For which I longingly await.

Some experiences
Brought reasons to elate,
While other lonely trials
Served to age and agitate.

To do it all again
And live to one-O-eight
Is still not time enough
For my energies to sate.

I wish I had more time
For my dreams to resonate,
To find success and happiness
Where sorrows would abate,

To see the world safe
From anger and from hate,
To know the planet's soul
Had man's soul for a mate.

I'd ask for one more day
To man illuminate
The beauty and the life
This space can emanate.

But forty-seven horses
Are waiting at the gate,
Rearing, dancing, charging,
And dragging me away.

Hope

Sparrows visit him,
dear statue of St. Francis,
whose hands are missing.

A Wish for a Better Planet

The story goes
that if you wish
for something badly enough,
you will get it.

If you wish your hardest,
spending every chance
on that one great wish
it <u>will</u> happen.

Since your thoughts
are all directed
towards that one goal,
you <u>make</u> it happen.

You wanted it enough
to wish for nothing else
and to waste no action
in the opposite direction.

But what if someone else's wish
were the exact opposite of yours
and he spared no wish
and wasted no action?

Whose dream would then come true
and whose would be lost - forever,
no matter how much it was wished for?

Ripples

The fish softly kisses
the glassy ceiling of his world.
His lips break through
to taste the air above.
His actions causing ripples
that spread across the pond.

An expanding ripple
lifts a water strider high
and carries it closer
to the shore
where a ravenous young frog
can reach it with his tongue,
almost.
The frog swallows the strider
as he loses his balance
and falls into the water.
His actions causing ripples
that spread across the pond.

A series of ripples
swells into the cattails
which sway back and forth,

greatly disturbing a redwing blackbird
declaring his territory.
He sings one last trill
and quickly takes flight
with a whirr of his wings
and a flash of yellow and red.
His actions causing ripples
that spread through the air.

A rippling air current
surprises a butterfly,
lifting her higher
and away from the pond.
Her beautiful wings
catch the afternoon light
and the eyes of a little girl
who falls in love with orange wings
seen against green leaves and blue sky
and who starts to learn about nature.
Her actions causing ripples
across her imagination.

One ripple carries her
through school to an illustrious career
in preservation and conservation
of the vanishing butterflies.

And as she succeeds
in rescuing this endangered beauty,
she saves also their habitats
such as the pond
with the fish and the strider,
the frog and the bird.
Whose actions cause ripples
that can change our world.

Snowy Owl

Snowy chicks huddle tightly,
weary from crying,
cold from the arctic breeze.
Fluttering noisily,
bare bellies hungry,
downy fuzz scant protection
in their open tundra nest.

Alone only for moments,
it seems like ages
against their three days
out of the egg.
Frightening - if they only knew,
but they are too young
and starving.

Alert to their cries
and close dangers both,
their mother returns
descending feet first,
tail spread wide,
cupped wing tips
lit by the sky.

Sunlight pours through
white feathers,
a luminous halo
greets her small chicks
as an angel from on high,
the snowy mother renests
to care for her young.

Raindrop

I imagine I'm a raindrop
sparkling on a windowpane.
I melt into buttery orange
as I nap inside a poppy.
I stretch myself across the sky
in the ruddy bands of sunset.
As a golden grain of sand,
I leave shore for open sea.
I wrap the world around me
and feel the currents in my soul.
I sense animal, plant, and water
course through my pulsing veins,
and become the flexing muscles
of a windmare
dashing through the rain.

Canopy Rain

The wind makes music
in the layered canopy
of the untamed forest,
where trees
spread their leaves overhead
and gently form both roof and rain.

The pines yearn to touch the sky,
stretching ever higher
to a point
unmoved by the wind,
except to shed needles
in the passing breeze.

The broadleaf trees below
do not stretch and thin so far.
Squat and wide
they quiver and sway
but hold tighter to their leaves
which sigh a song in the wind.

The wind harmonizes nature's
instruments
layered in the canopy.
It whispers through
and plays the song of rain
as pine needles shower softly
on the broadleafed roof below.

Silent Trees

The trees just stand there,
ever so still,
ever so quietly,
listening.

The world moves beneath them,
the sky changes above,
but the trees are still,
listening.

It seems they are wishing
that the rest of the world would quiet,
just for a moment,
so they could hear.

They are seeking an answer
to the question of their fate,
standing so patiently,
listening.

To hear what will become
of them and their world,
the trees stand silently,
waiting.

Rock-a-Bye Baby

Rock-a-bye baby,
in the tree top,
when the wind blows,
the cradle will rock.

And warm in her nest,
the baby will smile
and sleep, softly swaying,
cradled tree-style.

Outlived by a Wave

I stand
a minute of my days
on the ocean shore,
and watch these cresting waves
and listen to their roar.

I see the swell and rise
of awesome ocean peaks,
hear the voice of seagull cries
as water reaches sand it seeks.

Emerald horses froth and fall,
foamy manes are flying wild.
I blink just once through it all,
and stand there like a child.

This majestic ocean steed,
these transient crashing waves,
that fill my soulful need,
last but an instant of my days.

But I'm the instant creature here
along this ocean's coast.
A millisecond of an ocean's year
is all that I can boast.

This wave has lived far longer
than man or life itself,
it's existence and beauty stronger
than any I claim myself.

I stand
a minute of my days
and watch the ocean heave,
enchanted by these magic waves
still here when I must leave.

Each wave's life is so short,
but man's is shorter still.
Will the waves enjoy instants of <u>our</u> sort?
I can only hope they will.

Walk along the path
of a haiku, and see life
through the eyes of words.

A native of the West Coast and the Pacific Ocean, Maria Alexandria Boyd Paddock was born in Hawaii, raised in the San Francisco Bay Area, and has lived in the Puget Sound region of Washington for fourteen years. She now lives on a few wooded acres that get far more rain than they should with her husband and their cat, dog, horse, goat, turtle, and fish.

Maria holds degrees in psychology, zoology, and business administration (with a focus on environmental economics and sustainable development). Her abiding love of animals and the environment has led her into wildlife rescue and rehabilitation, veterinary work, and wetland stewardship. What she most wishes for is a world at peace, where people have enough to eat and homes to shelter them, where diversity is cherished and preserved, and where wild animals, trees, and wilderness lovers can thrive in their natural habitats. She hopes that her artistic expressions will inspire her readers to create such a world.